COMICS

for Social & Communicative Behavior

Vera Bernard-Opitz

illustrations by Andra Bernard

T0161577

COMICS FOR SOCIAL & COMMUNICATIVE BEHAVIOR

All marketing and publishing rights guaranteed to and reserved by:

FUTURE HORIZONS INC.

Toll-free: 800·489·0727 | Fax: 817·277·2270
www.FHautism.com | info@FHautism.com

Text © 2021 Vera Bernard-Opitz
Illustrations © 2021 Andra Bernard

The book was translated from its German original "Lernziel: Positives Sozial- und Kommunikationsver-halten." © Kohlhammer Gmbh, Stuttgart

All rights reserved.
Printed in the USA.

No part of this product may be reproduced in any manner whatsoever without written permission of Future Horizons, except in the case of brief quotations embodied in reviews.

ISBN: 9781949177671

Introduction!

Appropriate social and communicative behavior is a fundamental concern for parents and teachers of schoolchildren. Children and teenagers should be able to move in a safe and socially successful manner through their school years despite changing family culture, their high activity level and a lack of insight into the consequences of their behavior. One would also hope that they develop a positive character and good values related to human rights and social responsibility along the way. The most important long-term goal, however, is that they become content, kind and successful fellow human beings.

Historically, religion once had a distinct impact on the attitudes and behaviors of individuals, communities and societies. Rules were clear, and a "good conscience," an overseeing God or fear of eternal punishment enforced moral guidelines. During the last ᵗwenty years, social changes have occurred which have shifted ᵗs from traditional religious values to personal happiness and "wellness." Teachers, and even employers, complain that they must focus on ethics and social values, as they often are not sufficiently practiced at home or in the community. Commitment, a positive work attitude, politeness, respect and a sense of responsibility and reliability can no longer be taken for granted from students entering school.

This Social Cartoon Curriculum illustrates more than 120 goals for developing positive personality features, adequate social behavior and communicative competence. Ideas for long- and short-term goals have been selected from existing school programs, general education of values, and the wishes of parents, teachers and employers. A precursor of the book was the *Cartoon and Script Curriculum for Training Social Behavior and Communication*, which is aimed at children with Autism Spectrum Disorders (Bernard-Opitz, 2014).

Since the 80s, the Positive Behavior Support *(PBS)* movement has had an important influence on the development of values and binding educational strategies in the US. In the beginning, PBS was developed on the basis of behavioral strategies to prevent problem behavior (Dunlap, 2009; Zuna & McDougall, 2004; Carr et al, 1999; Koegel, Koegel & Dunlap, 2001). Schools for children with challenging behavior or disabilities were supposed to use Positive Behavior Intervention Support (PBIS) to enable life success and active participation in community activities. Since then, the strategy has been expanded to develop core family and cultural values as well as a positive school culture. Both typical and special needs students from kindergarten onward are taught specific skills, such as communication, problem solving, critical thinking and teamwork (McGinnis, 2005; Baker, 2004). A specific number of expectations is determined, which are actively taught to all students and tested for their effects. Each school can select its most important set of values. The following STAR Program is a Californian example of such a PBS program. During the first school weeks, students in grades 5–8 are introduced to the concepts below. This has the advantage of having rules set from the very beginning, which can be referred to in later years. Under the

STAR Program, each student receives small stars on a star card, which can be turned in at the end of the month for small surprises. The abbreviation for "STAR" stands for the following teaching goals:

S - Safety first

T – There and ready

A – Act responsibly

R – Respect self and others

The Carson private schools have a comparable educational plan. Every morning, the students make the pledge of allegiance to the American flag and select an additional promise regarding their personal character goals. Following this, they must each promise their specific goal with a handshake to the school principal. During the principal's tours around the campus, the principal asks individual students what value they currently focus on.

Education in human values and character formation are also important goals in international schools. Responsibility, prosocial behavior and team skills tend to be top targets. Often these goals are not directly taught but integrated in the school day. While there are many curricula and teaching material for the typical school subjects, material for social behavior and character foundation is hard to find. Here the following cartoon curriculum tries to provide a clear learning structure and ideas on what to teach. The cartoons can be used for project days, afternoon school or substitute teaching hours.

Typically developing and special needs students can be taught or be reminded of positive behavior, which is important in school, home and later at the work place. The explicit visual presentation of behavior valued by society can also be useful for inclusion classes. Through simple scripts and drawings, even newly immigrated students can benefit from learning their new home country's values, rules and expectations. In addition, the thought and speech bubbles can help with learning common language scripts.

The cartoons show simple problem situations, which can either be solved in a positive or a negative way. Illustrations give a choice between these two options. An additional light bulb indicates that the student can alternatively come up with his own solutions. It is obvious that the pictured examples should only serve as ideas to introduce the respective goals. In addition, students should be involved in discussions, role-play and video-modeling to learn comparable individually relevant goals (in more detail, see Bernard-Opitz, 2016).

This book can be used for kindergarten and elementary school children. In addition, adolescents and adults can also be reminded that behavior is always a selection between a "good choice" and a behavior, which in hindsight may not have shown one's "best self."

I hope the cartoons are fun and carry the message that value education and character formation can be taught in a direct and entertaining way in kindergartens, elementary schools and beyond. The presented book should only be considered a small first step!

— *Vera Bernard-Opitz, Ph.D.*
Hildesheim & Irvine, March 2021

The following book shows 125 cartoons which focus on the STAR program, as well as eight long-term goals such as the *development of friendship, responsibility, optimism, self-control,* and *communicative competence*. Long-term goals *(LTGs)* are divided into different short-term goals *(STGs)*, which are represented by four cartoons each. Most examples target specific goals but can also be applied to others.

To develop the LTGs of "Popularity, Courtesy and Friendship Skills," STGs focus on following instructions, paying attention to the perspective of others, showing consideration, being helpful and being modest. The LTG "Optimism" is illustrated by cartoons of children who persist on difficult tasks and don't give up.

The cartoons present simple problem situations which can either be solved appropriately or inappropriately. The illustrations help to make a wise decision between two possible alternatives. In addition, a *light bulb* indicates the students' own contribution to a possible solution.

Before each chapter, LTGs are introduced with a table summarizing the respective STGs. Correct responses are noted with a plus, faulty answers with a minus, and not quite sufficient performances with a diagonal line. Corresponding notes can be made in the table.

It goes without saying that the examples chosen should merely be suggestions for introducing the listed goals. It is therefore important to develop comparable short-term goals and generalize the teaching targets through additional discussions, role-plays and video-modeling (Bernard-Opitz, 2016).

A) Examples of developing values and social behavior at schools

It is just after 8 AM at a public middle school in Irvine, an open school without doors in each classroom. The students sit at their desks and patiently wait for the lesson to start. Two twelve-year-old students try to pass through the entrance, talking quite loudly and shoving each other. A teacher stops both of them and tells them to walk down the hallway the way they have been told: quietly and separately. The students comply with guilty faces.

For some people, this real example may be a horrifying scenario of a students' suppressed school life. In contrast, for other teachers and students, a school without high noise levels and risky shoving in the hallways or on stairs may be a way to prevent stress and burnout.

The following is an example of a school-wide program that tries to prevent problems through positive behavior support (PBS). The teaching strategies explain the above student and teacher behavior, which happened at a middle school in Irvine.

The abbreviation **STAR** stands for **S**afety first at school and in the community, **T**here and ready, **A**ct responsibly and **R**espect self and others.

Individual schools can adapt the above learning goals to the needs of their students. Lately, the abbreviation "T" in the STAR-program has been changed to "**T**houghtful communication," which is also an important social goal for elementary and middle school students. The above curriculum is embedded in a special teacher training program that focuses on the prevention of students' problems through the modification of teachers' behaviors (Simpson & Allday, 2008).

STAR Program

- · S = Safety first
- · T = There and ready
- · A = Act responsibly
- · R = Respect self and others

Safety first is an important message, because schools should be safe places for students. Sadly, safety has decreased in the past years, especially in the United States. In 2018, since the shooting at the Columbine School in 1999, more than 187,000 American students had experienced gunfights during school hours (Chiu & Horton, 2018).

According to an insurance report in Germany in 2017, about 1.18 million school accidents have been documented. More than half of the accidents happen during physical education classes and about a quarter during recess, so these activities should be focus points for prevention. (*https://www.dguv.de/de/zahlen-fakten/ schuelerunfallgeschehen/index.jsp*). Thirty-eight students had a fatal accident on the way to or from school. This sad statistic should be another reason for preventive safety measures.

The cartoons below were created to help students be better prepared for school expectations. The following examples are suggestions for similar situations with comparable goals of pupil and school needs. Several examples have been selected out of the possible scenarios students experience, such as exhibiting *safe behavior* while riding their bike, being alert when a ball is approaching, or jumping without first checking the pool-side reserved for swimmers. Keeping a safe distance behind swings can prevent accidents on school grounds.

Being *There and Ready* for learning is another goal in STAR-schools, including behaviors such as arriving on time in class or coming back from the bathroom and recess on time.

Disturbance in class and inappropriate use of cell phones can be illustrated by cartoons, role-playing games or video modeling. Being alert also means speaking your mind if someone makes a mistake or contradicting someone when their opinion is wrong or questionable.

Acting responsibly has different faces, such as getting help if someone's nose is bleeding or if he has other injuries. Being an "honest finder" is another example, like the student who follows the school rules. Picking up trash should not be the job of the janitor, but should also involve the students. From the beginning of their school experience students should learn about expectations at school.

Respecting self and others can be instructed and reinforced through alerting appropriate behavior towards others. Students should show their best behavior and not distract others or prevent learning through loud noise, clowning, bullying or disruptive behavior.

Examples of positive alternative behavior are pictured through cartoons. Teachers can add discussions from current problem situations and transpose these into role-play. Cartoon examples of tolerance towards minorities like Muslim students, students who think differently and disabled students can be used to start a class conversation.

The **STAR Program** shows overlaps in the following chapters, which refer to positive personal characteristics and appropriate social and communicative behavior. The following program is divided into two sections: The STAR-Program can be completed within the first two weeks of school and should involve the entire school, including the students' parents. The second and main part of the program can be conducted throughout the school year.

S – Safety first
- Wearing a helmet
- Paying attention at the swings
- Jumping into the pool
- Being careful with strangers

T – There and ready

- Arriving on time to class
- Paying attention during physical education
- Not interrupting in class
- Doing your homework without distractions

A – Act responsibly

- Helping a classmate with a nosebleed
- Handing back a lost wallet
- No littering in public places
- Not disturbing neighbors

R – Respect self and others

- No burping
- Respecting classmates from different cultures
- Not excluding people with disabilities
- Respecting the privacy of others

Chart 1: STAR Program

NAME OF STUDENT:_____	CARTOON	ROLE-PLAYING	VIDEO-MODELING	DISCUSSION
DATE				
S – Safety first				
• Wearing a helmet				
• Paying attention at the swings				
• Jumping into the pool				
• Being careful with strangers				
T – There and ready				
• Arriving on time to class				
• Paying attention during physical education				
• Not interrupting in class				
• Doing your homework without distractions				

NAME OF STUDENT: _____	CARTOON	ROLE-PLAYING	VIDEO-MODELING	DISCUSSION
DATE				
A – Act responsibly				
• Helping a classmate with a nosebleed				
• Handing back a lost wallet				
• Not littering in public places				
• Not disturbing neighbors				
R – Respect self and others				
• No burping				
• Respecting classmates from different cultures				
• Not excluding people with disabilities				
• Respecting the privacy of others				

You want to ride your bike.
What is safe behavior?

It is recess and you run outside behind the swing.
What is safe behavior?

**LTG STAR
S – Safety
First**

You are at the pool and want to jump from the 5-meter board.
What is safe behavior?

School is out and your mother told you to wait for her in front of the school. A stranger asks if you want to see her kittens.
What is safe behavior?

It is almost 8:00 AM and your class is about to start.
What do you think/say/do?

You receive a message in the middle of your soccer game.
What do you think/say/do?

Your teacher wants you to pay attention, but you keep talking to your neighbor.
What do you think/say/do?

You have a lot of homework to do, but your cell phone rings.
What do you think/say/do?

LTG STAR
A – Act
Responsibly

Your classmate's nose is bleeding.
What do you think/say/do?

You find a wallet with money inside.
What do you think/say/do?

You finished your food.
What do you think/say/do?

You are playing soccer with your friend at noon (nap time).
What do you think/say/do?

LTG STAR
R – Respect
Self and
Others

While talking to your neighbor, a burp escapes your mouth.
What do you think/say/do?

One of your classmates is wearing a headscarf.
What do you think/say/do?

LTG STAR
R – Respect
Self and
Others

Your classmates see a child with autistic behavior.
What do you think/say/do?

You see Tom looking over the stall in the bathroom.
What do you think/say/do?

A) Goals for positive social behavior!

An elderly lady enters the train compartment, where a boy of about six years sits next to the window. She asks him kindly if she can hang her jacket next to him, and he refuses. She is shocked by his answer and searches for an alternative hook on the opposite window. She keeps glancing at the boy with a lack of understanding.

Being polite means interacting respectfully with others to avoid bringing them into an uncomfortable situation. Elderly and weak people and people in higher positions should especially be handled with respect. Maybe the lady's kind question was misunderstood by the boy. Did he really not want the jacket next to him or did he want to prove his contradictions skills to an elderly person? The lady was surprised by the boy's answer, since she didn't act disrespectfully towards older people in her own childhood. Nowadays it is likely that she has seen even small children making decisions, even if they can't yet understand the consequences. In any case, a friendly contact has come to an abrupt end.

Arthur Schopenhauer defines **being polite** as follows:

> Being polite is a verbal and non-verbal behavior which is a normal component of regular interactions. Its purpose is to bring benefits to another person indirectly or to spare them embarrassment. *https://de.wikipedia.org/wiki/Höflichkeit.*

In current times, bullying, hate speech and aggression have become an everyday life experience. Therefore, many wish that a "good character education" and empathetic interactions with others would return. Most students have to be reminded to use simple courtesy phrases such as greetings, requests and thank. Therefore, long-term goals such as "being polite and making friends" must be targeted.

The current book shows exemplary cartoons on various **short-term goals (STG)**. These demonstrate steps in a kinder interaction style.

For parents, teachers and therapists, it is a relief when children follow **demands** immediately, such as when they hear a joyful "I'm coming," "I heard you," or "I'll be there in five minutes" after calling them. It is also helpful when children don't need repeated requests to complete certain duties but instead write their own to-do lists. *(STG 1). Empathy* is recognizing what others feel, which is the foundation of successful teams and professional success (Goleman, 1995). In former times, children learned through puppets and role-play to take another's perspective and to develop their sensitivity to social contexts. It can be hypothesized that the recent increase of apps and computers prevents children from social learning. Through cartoons of social problem-solving, we try to undo the above unfortunate developments.

Empathy is recognizing what others feel, which is the foundation of successful teams and professional success (Goleman, 1995). In former times, children learned through puppets and role-play to take another's perspective and to develop their sensitivity to social contexts. It can be hypothesized that the recent increase of apps and computers prevents children from social learning. Through cartoons of social problem solving, we try to undo the above unfortunate developments.

In the beginning, understanding *physical perspectives* must be targeted. Children must learn not to run into others, to block their view nor to intrude into the space of peers *(STG 2)*.

Another even more difficult teaching goal is *to empathize, to be helpful and to be considerate towards others*. The following short-term goals are examples of being helpful to your parents, class-mates, siblings or elderly people *(STG 2, 3 and 4)*.

Being humble, for example, appears to be a lost virtue. Many teenagers currently seem dependent on Facebook likes for being the coolest, most popular or most interesting person. However, this is no guarantee of a true friend. The following cartoons exemplify humbleness as an important training target to make friends.

LTG 1 Being kind and popular and making friends

STG 1 Following instructions

- Cleaning up your room
- Coming when called
- Coming home when it is dark
- Checking off the To-Do-List

STG 2 Considering the perspectives of others

- Being careful on stairs
- Comforting your neighbor
- Supporting your friend
- Offering an umbrella in the rain

STG 3 Helping and respecting others

- Letting younger siblings win
- Offering a seat to someone on the bus
- Letting older people go ahead at the cash register
- Showing a new student around school

STG 4 Being helpful

- Helping a classmate with his homework
- Helping your dad with washing the car
- Defending someone who is bullied
- Helping your neighbor with the trash

STG 5 Being humble

- Not bragging about your skills
- Not bragging about your possession
- Not making someone feel inferior
- Being humble when invited to a restaurant

Chart 2: LTG Being kind and popular and making friends

NAME OF STUDENT: _____	CARTOON	ROLE-PLAYING	VIDEO-MODELING	DISCUSSION
DATE				
LTG 1: Being kind and popular and making friends				
STG 1 Following instructions				
• Cleaning up your room				
• Coming when called				
• Coming home when it is dark				
• Checking off the To-Do-List				
STG 2 Considering the perspectives of others				
• Being careful on stairs				
• Comforting your neighbor				
• Supporting your friend				
• Offering an umbrella in the rain				

NAME OF STUDENT: _____	CARTOON	ROLE-PLAYING	VIDEO-MODELING	DISCUSSION
DATE				
STG 3 Helping and respecting others				
• Letting younger siblings win				
• Offering a seat to someone on the bus				
• Letting older people go ahead at the cash register				
• Showing a new student around school				
STG 4 Being helpful				
• Helping a classmate with his homework				
• Helping your dad with washing the car				
• Defending someone who is bullied				
• Helping your neighbor with the trash				
STG 5 Being humble				
• Not bragging about your skills				
• Not bragging about your possession				
• Not making someone feel inferior				
• Being humble when invited to a restaurant				

LTG 1
Being kind and popular and making friends

1.1
Following instructions

Your mother wants you to clean up your room.
What do you think/say/do?

You are called for dinner, but you are playing a game.
What do you think/say/do?

LTG 1
Being kind
and popular
and making
friends

1.1
Following
instructions

You want to play soccer longer, but it is getting dark.
What do you think/say/do?

You have to finish your to-do list before you can play with your friends.
What do you think/say/do?

LTG 1
Being kind
and popular
and making
friends

1.2
Considering
the perspec-
tives of others

It is recess time and you start running down the stairs.
What do you think/say/do?

Your neighbor received a bad grade.
What do you think/say/do?

LTG 1
Being kind
and popular
and making
friends

1.2
Considering
the perspec-
tives of others

Your friend tells you that he has his first date today.
What do you think/say/do?

It is raining very hard and your classmate is walking in front of you.
What do you think/say/do?

LTG 1
Being kind and popular and making friends

1.3
Helping and respecting others

You and your younger brother are playing his favorite card game, and he is eager to win.
What do you think/say/do?

A pregnant woman gets on the bus and wants to sit down.
What do you think/say/do?

The man behind you at the cashier only has one item.
What do you think/say/do?

There is a new student at school, and your teacher wants someone to show him around.
What do you think/say/do?

LTG 1
Being kind
and popular
and making
friends

1.4
Being
helpful

Your neighbor does not understand the homework.
What do you think/say/do?

Your dad is washing the car, even though he had a long day.
What do you think/say/do?

LTG 1
Being kind
and popular
and making
friends

1.4
Being helpful

Your classmates are bullying a peer on the playground.
What do you think/say/do?

You see that your neighbor needs help with the trash.
What do you think/say/do?

You got a better grade than your classmate, who is very happy with his B-.
What do you think/say/do?

Your classmate tells you that his dad bought the new BMW.
What do you think/say/do?

LTG 1
Being kind
and popular
and making
friends

1.5
Being humble

Two of your friends are taking selfies and bragging about how good the iPhone is.
What do you think/say/do?

Your friend's dad has invited you to an expensive restaurant.
What do you think/say/do?

While introducing our children at the German school in Singapore, we proudly showed the principal their previous work from a local Montessori kindergarten. They had already learned to spell, write short words and add numbers. I wanted to know how we could prepare them for the primary school. The vice principal looked at their work and commented, "It is better for your children to forget everything they have learned, because they need to learn to do their best independent of praise from others. An example: if they build an excavator, it should be the best excavator they could possibly come up with, regardless of feedback from others.

It may be argued that the vice principal's behavior reflects the different views on teaching and praise in the German and Singaporean school systems. Obviously, he expects independent perfect work. In Germany, conscientiousness and trustworthiness are expected from not only teachers, but also employers and workers.

Being reliable is often mentioned as one of the most demanded personal characteristics in fields such as medicine and the pharmaceutical and automotive industries. Even without supervision, an employee must be trusted to work diligently and conscientiously.

Again, it is not easy to operationalize this long-term goal (LTG) nor to develop a series of related short-term goals (STG). We can only show selected behaviors within this category. As in the previous chapters, the following cartoons should only be considered examples from a vast array of possibilities. Parents and teachers are encouraged to develop comparable choices.

Respecting rules is one major behavioral goal in middle school. Students are expected to arrive on time, work peacefully and focus on tasks. Many rules are not explicitly explained, such as returning from breaks on time, getting dressed for physical education, putting up your chair when class is over, not using your cell phone during class and not eating in class, and not speaking when the teacher is speaking.

At some schools, most rules are demonstrated through posters in class or token systems, where students earn points for a reward at the end of the week. As mentioned before, it is helpful to introduce specific rules explicitly at the beginning of the school year.

Following *explicit or implicit rules*, such as verbal or written rules, is required when showing respect to parents, teachers or other authorities. Students learn to respect the janitor, coach, pastor, salesman and police as they also learn to pay attention in traffic and to obey the traffic signs. *(STG 2.1)*

At home, as in school, children should be instructed to do what they have promised. This may include doing homework, packing their school bag the night before, or preparing for a group presentation. *(STG 2.2)*

In addition, children as well as adults must follow many expectations, such as doing small household chores. It is also polite to respond to text messages or stay in contact if something strange has happened or if one is unable to stick to a promise. Parents tend to rely on their children to show safe behaviors, such as locking their bikes or the front door. *(STG 2.3)*

Taking over **responsibility** is another component in becoming a reliable adult. It starts with taking care of pets, younger siblings, or weak or disabled family members or classmates.

Turning off lights, separating garbage and using food, paper and recyclables wisely are additional examples of being a responsible person.

Being on time or having good time management are important characteristics for successful schooling. These features are also central in several jobs. Arriving on time for the bus, train, or class or from recess is a behavior children need to learn. Their free time or social events must be planned on time so that exams, projects or birthday invitations will be successful.

Conscientiousness is another important trait of a reliable student or employee. Attention to detail as well as studious and accurate work can prevent negative consequences, such as criticism or loss of privileges. For children who get easily distracted by social media, this might be difficult.

LTG 2 Being responsible and reliable

STG 1 Respecting instructions

- Respecting school decisions
- Respecting behavior rules
- Respecting authority figures
- Respecting public rules

STG 2 Doing what you promised

- Doing your homework
- Answering text messages
- Packing your schoolbag on time
- Feeding the pets

STG 3 Doing what is expected

- Writing an essay
- Unloading the dishwasher
- Putting dirty clothes in the basket
- Locking the front door

STG 4 Taking responsibility for others and the environment

- Babysitting
- Taking a classmate in a wheelchair along
- Not throwing away food
- Turning off the light

STG 5 Time management and being on time

- Not showering for too long
- Being on time for an internship
- Sending birthday invitations on time
- Not missing the train

Chart 3: LTG 2 Being responsible and reliable

NAME OF STUDENT: _____	CARTOON	ROLE-PLAYING	VIDEO-MODELING	DISCUSSION
DATE				
LTG 2: Being responsible and reliable				
STG 1 Respecting instructions				
• Respecting school decisions				
• Respecting behavior rules				
• Respecting authority figures				
• Respecting public rules				
STG 2 Doing what you promised				
• Doing your homework				
• Answering text messages				
• Packing your schoolbag on time				
• Feeding the pets				

NAME OF STUDENT: _____	CARTOON	ROLE-PLAYING	VIDEO-MODELING	DISCUSSION
DATE				
STG 3 Doing what is expected				
• Writing an essay				
• Unloading the dishwasher				
• Putting dirty clothes in the basket				
• Locking the front door				
STG 4 Taking responsibility for others and the environment				
• Babysitting				
• Bringing a classmate in a wheelchair along				
• Not throwing away food				
• Turning off the light				
STG 5. Time management and being on time				
• Not showering for too long				
• Being on time for an internship				
• Sending birthday invitations on time				
• Not missing the train				

LTG 2
Being
responsible
and reliable

2.1
Respecting
instructions

Your friend does not want to go to class.
What do you think/say/do?

Your teacher wants you to spit out your gum.
What do you think/say/do?

LTG 2
Being
responsible
and reliable

2.1
Respecting
instructions

You get caught while stealing sweets at the store.
What do you think/say/do?

You notice the sign that indicates that there is no swimming allowed in the lake.
What do you think/say/do?

LTG 2
Being
responsible
and reliable

2.2 Doing
what you
promised

You wanted to correct tomorrow's homework.
What do you think/say/do?

Your mom wants you to answer the messages.
What do you think/say/do?

LTG 2
Being
responsible
and reliable

2.2 Doing
what you
promised

You are cuddled up in bed, but your school bag is not packed.
What do you think/say/do?

Your mother wants you to feed the dog.
What do you think/say/do?

LTG 2
Being
responsible
and reliable

2.3
Doing what
is expected

You have to write an essay, but it seems very hard.
What do you think/say/do?

Your mother wants you to clear out the dishwasher.
What do you think/say/do?

LTG 2
Being
responsible
and reliable

2.3
Doing what
is expected

You are supposed to put your clothes into the bin.
What do you think/say/do?

You are in a rush but should still lock the front door.
What do you think/say/do?

LTG 2
Being
responsible
and reliable

2.4
Taking
responsibility
for others
and the
environment

Can you watch your little sister today?

I don't have any time!

Of course!

You are asked to babysit your little sister for the night.
What do you think/say/do?

Come on, let's go to the race! It's starting soon!

Let's bring Tim along.

Let's go!

Your friend picks you up for the school race.
What do you think/say/do?

LTG 2
Being
responsible
and reliable

2.4
Taking
responsibility
for others
and the
environment

The pizza was too much for you and you will not be able to finish it.
What do you think/say/do?

You are getting ready for school in the bathroom with all the lights on.
What do you think/say/do?

It is getting late for school and you still need to shower.
What do you think/say/do?

It is your first day of your internship.
What do you think/say/do?

LTG 2
Being responsible and reliable

2.5
Time management and being on time

Your birthday is in two weeks, and you still have to hand out your invitations.
What do you think/say/do?

The train is about to depart, but you want to buy a Coke.
What do you think/say/do?

After his team has lost the soccer match, eleven-year-old Jimmy sits crying on the grass. He grumbles, "We would have won if I'd kicked the penalty shot! We will never win with such a stupid team!"

Many children, youngsters and adults find it difficult to lose, especially when they are competitive and try to be better than the rest. They only identify with their team in the case of success. This can become a problem during P.E class, teamwork in school or later in working life.

Teamwork means working together and respecting each other's skills and ideas.

Arrogant behavior, inappropriate dominance or withdrawal can lead to conflicts. In order to avoid these situations, teams should develop trust and tolerance of each other and work on joint problem solving. It is important to support each other so that risks can be shared and personal failures don't lead to a loss of face.

Pre-schoolers should learn to work on common goals; they should be able to lose or to negotiate conflicts. Fair play can be practiced through board games or sports. In the following cartoons, we have selected a few examples to demonstrate underlying components of team skills (see Table 4).

Working together towards a goal is based on cooperative play. At the age of three to four, this skill develops and refines itself during school years. Even simple turn-taking when rolling a ball back to where the playmate is can be a first step to becoming a team partner. Children must attend to their peers and adjust their behavior accordingly. Learning how to deal with conflicts within a group is another hurdle *(STG 3.1)*.

It is not easy to accept critique or to revise your behavior and your opinion if the majority of your team has a different opinion. It is even more difficult to stand behind your team and to admit mistakes (as in the vignette above) or to be caught making mistakes or fooling around (Example: Puddle) *(STG 3.2)*.

Children often don't want to disappoint their peer group but must make compromises to meet the conflicting needs of parents, teachers, coaches or friends *(STG 3.3)*.

A team doesn't function well if a team member is unfair towards others. Fair play and fair distribution of tasks are important components of team skills.

Members of a team can decide on the team leader and the individual assignment of each member. The frequency, time and location of meetings are also important decision points. If the goal of the team is a concert, a competition or an exam, time management skills are also useful *(STG 3.4)*.

LTG 3 Having good team skills

STG 1 Setting team goals

- Following instructions during P.E class
- Accepting team decisions
- Giving compliments to team players
- Participating actively in groups

STG 2 Accepting criticism

- Accepting critical arguments
- Accepting critique about behavior
- Accepting negative feedback about appearance
- Accepting responsibility for mistakes in a group

STG 3 Suggesting or accepting compromises

- Choice of restaurants
- Choice of movies
- When parents restrict computer time
- When going out late at night

STG 4 Being fair

- Dividing tasks fairly
- Giving everyone a chance
- Playing without cheating
- Clarifying disputes

Chart 4: LTG 3 Having good team skills

NAME OF STUDENT: _____	CARTOON	ROLE-PLAYING	VIDEO-MODELING	DISCUSSION
DATE				
LTG 3 Having good team skills				
STG 1 Setting team-goals				
• Following instructions during P.E class				
• Accepting team decisions				
• Giving compliments to team players				
• Participating actively in groups				
STG 2 Accepting criticism				
• Accepting critical arguments				
• Accepting critique about behavior				
• Accepting negative feedback about appearance				
• Accepting responsibility for mistakes in a group				

NAME OF STUDENT: _____	CARTOON	ROLE-PLAYING	VIDEO-MODELING	DISCUSSION
DATE				
STG 3 Suggesting or accepting compromises				
• Choice of restaurants				
• Choice of movies				
• When parents restrict computer time				
• When going out late at night				
STG 4 Being fair				
• Dividing tasks fairly				
• Giving everyone a chance				
• Playing without cheating				
• Clarifying disputes				

LTG 3
Having good
team skills

3.1
Setting
team goals

You are playing basketball with your friend, and he wants you to pass the ball.
What do you think/say/do?

You are not allowed to play on the school's top team.
What do you think/say/do?

LTG 3
Having good
team skills

3.1
Setting
team goals

Your friends select a music piece for the school show that you don't like.
What do you think/say/do?

You are supposed to help your group with the poster.
What do you think/say/do?

You recall wrongly that there is P.E. today, but everyone else reminds you that it was rescheduled.
What do you think/say/do?

Your tennis trainer catches you smoking.
What do you think/say/do?

LTG 3
Having good
team skills

3.2
Accepting
criticism

You arrive at school with dirty clothes, and your peers gossip about you.
What do you think/say/do?

Your dad is upset about the puddle in the hallway and wants to know
who did it.
What do you think/say/do?

LTG 3
Having good
team skills

3.3
Suggesting
or accepting
compromises

Your team wants to go to McDonald's, but you want to go to Burger King instead.
What do you think/say/do?

Your friends want to watch a movie that you already know, but you want to watch a new movie.
What do you think/say/do?

LTG 3
Having good
team skills

3.3
Suggesting
or accepting
compromises

Your mom wants you to stop playing games with your friends.
What do you think/say/do?

Your mom will be worried if you take the train all alone to your
friend's birthday party.
What do you think/say/do?

You and your group have to do a PowerPoint presentation, and you want Mark to do most of the work.
What do you think/say/do?

Kamu wants to be goalie but misses the ball several times.
What do you think/say/do?

LTG 3
Having good
team skills

3.4
Being fair

You are playing a board game, and one of the players claims that you are cheating.
What do you think/say/do?

Anna never showed up for the rehearsal of the Christmas story, but she still wants to be part of the play.
What do you think/say/do?

Several years ago, I directed an early intervention program for children with Down's Syndrome in Singapore. It was not easy to keep track of twenty Chinese, Malayan and Indian children who were between 6–24 months. Memorizing their unfamiliar names, such as Hsia Yun, Yit Lai and Kian Woon, was difficult. When two parents introduced their child with the name "Joy," I was relieved, since that name was easy to remember, but I was also surprised. They explained that they had first been disappointed to have a child with Down's Syndrome. After a few days of mourning, they decided to make her the center of joy in the family. Joy developed into a happy child who was a true enrichment for her parents and for many people in the early intervention center.

It is certainly admirable that the parents changed their attitude towards their six-month-old infant into an optimistic outlook. Instead of anticipating all the health, scholastic and social difficulties, they expected a life that would bring joy, and this expectation was met. They were by no means naïve about the development of children with Down Syndrome but certainly wise to approach the not-so-easy situation optimistically.

Optimism is the expectation that developments will be positive. This is reflected in the sayings, "This world is the best world ever!" (Leibniz) and "A glass is half full rather than half empty." Having an optimistic view helps with handling daily life events. An optimistic attitude also goes along with better handling of social relations events and improved mental health. Even if optimism has a genetic component, a positive family environment helps those who are not blessed with a positive disposition.

An optimistic attitude can help with daily stress situations, such as being tailgated by someone who is in a hurry on the highway. Instead of being agitated about the driver, one should consider that he might have a good reason for his speeding. The following fictitious assumption might be a helpful one: "His wife is about to give birth, and he wants to be on time." Even if these reasons are questionable, they might help against the negative effect of so-called "poisonous thoughts" on psychological wellbeing. In order to contribute to long-term health, it seems important to teach children positive thinking. The following STGs show examples of everyday problem situations *(see table 5)*.

Not giving up means to keep going even if it gets hard. When practicing vocabulary, learning an instrument or trying to swim, not giving up on the first failure is a good recipe for success. In the beginning, it is often difficult to play the flute or the piano, to walk on stilts or to ride a unicycle, but constant practice usually pays off. While some children find it difficult to anticipate success and engage in repeated efforts, others keep trying. In the long term, being proud of one's achievements as well as being praised for an accomplishment can contribute to a positive self-image. This can be helpful for educational, professional and social development *(STG 4.1)*.

It is difficult for not only students *to think positively about themselves or others*, but also apparently adults. We tend to castigate ourselves and attribute negative motives towards co-workers, neighbors, children and partners. Some thoughts can escalate quickly from a slight instance of forgetfulness, such as when one is asked to buy an ingredient for dinner or does not receive a response to text messages and quickly reaches the conclusions "This person doesn't think about my wishes" or "I am not worth a thought." In the long term, negative thinking can make you sick and trigger a depressive mood.

Practicing positive thoughts as early as possible helps to overcome the mentioned "poisonous thoughts." For your mental health, it is better to relate problems to the here and now than to "eternity." Not winning a race *once* doesn't mean to *never* win a race. It is always possible to meet someone who has a grumpy day and bumps into you, excludes you or teases you. Again, it is wiser to find a situational explanation for such behavior and to respond with positive serenity.

Related to positive thoughts about yourself and others is the tendency to *give yourself and others a second chance*. Cartoon examples pictured for enabling opportunities are involving an immigrant peer during soccer, tolerating younger siblings during play and taking your grandma out for ice cream *(STG 4.3)*.

Altruistic behavior can have a positive effect on self-satisfaction. Some parents encourage daily self-reflections when bringing their children to bed, asking, "What went well?" or "What can you do better tomorrow?" Later, as teenagers, they might look back and think about their choices. "Did I put sufficient effort into my work and social life?" or "Did I miss chances by making negative decisions, such as clowning/chaos/drug groups instead of learning, community or hobby groups?"

LTG 4 Optimism

STG 1 Never give up

- Practicing swimming
- Keep going when physical effort is needed
- Practicing a new language
- Asking for help (flying a kite)

STG 2 Thinking positively about yourself and others

- Don't give up when losing
- Don't take revenge on someone
- Don't make yourself to be the outsider
- Practicing your handwriting

STG 3 Taking advantage of your own chance and giving others a chance

- Integrating minorities
- Including younger siblings
- Making wise decisions
- Including older people

Chart 5: LTG 4 Optimism

NAME OF STUDENT: _____	CARTOON	ROLE-PLAYING	VIDEO-MODELING	DISCUSSION
DATE				
LTG 4 Optimism				
STG 1 Never give up				
• Practicing swimming				
• Keep going when physical effort is needed				
• Practicing a new language				
• Asking for help (flying a kite)				
STG 2 Thinking positively about yourself and others				
• Don't give up when losing				
• Don't take revenge on someone				
• Don't make yourself to be the outsider				
• Practicing your handwriting				

NAME OF STUDENT: _____	CARTOON	ROLE-PLAYING	VIDEO-MODELING	DISCUSSION
DATE				
STG 3 Taking advantage of your own chance and giving others a chance				
• Integrating minorities				
• Including younger siblings				
• Making wise decisions				
• Including older people				

LTG 4
Optimism

4.1
Never give up

During swimming lessons, you are always the last one.
What do you think/say/do?

You are on a scout mission, but you are exhausted.
What do you think/say/do?

LTG 4
Optimism

4.1
Never give up

You cannot really understand your classmate, because his English is not so good.
What do you think/say/do?

All the children are letting their kites fly, but yours is not even getting off the ground.
What do you think/say/do?

LTG 4
Optimism

4.2
Thinking
positively
about
yourself
and others

You made it through the finish line first.
What do you think/say/do?

Someone bumped into you on purpose.
What do you think/say/do?

LTG 4
Optimism

4.2
Thinking
positively
about
yourself
and others

You were not invited to a classmate's birthday.
What do you think/say/do?

Your neighbor says that nobody can read your handwriting.
What do you think/say/do?

LTG 4
Optimism

4.3
Taking
advantage
of your own
chance and
giving others
a chance

You are playing soccer with your friends, and you see a refugee standing on the side.
What do you think/say/do?

Your little brother likes to come into your room, but he gets your toys mixed up.
What do you think/say/do?

LTG 4
Optimism

4.3
Taking
advantage
of your own
chance and
giving others
a chance

You are debating whether to go to the smokers or to the ones learning for the exam.
What do you think/say/do?

You want to eat an ice cream with your best friend, and your grandma is sitting in the living room by herself.
What do you think/say/do?

During an internship in an orphanage in Romania, I observed a one-year-old child who tried to hold on to the wall to learn how to walk. Again and again he slipped away from the smooth wall, but giving up was not an option. He finally managed to take one step and smiled broadly.

Obviously, the boy didn't stop believing in his own strength and the idea of walking. The repeated falls did not hinder him but instead increased his efforts. Children like this boy have a difficult start in life. However, they may have learned hardiness, which helps manage daily problems through the belief in their own strength.

Resilience is the ability of children, adolescents and adults not to be discouraged by setbacks, but instead to become stronger for handling new challenges. While sickness, accidents, trauma or loss of a loved one might pose a serious health risk for some individuals, others might develop healthy coping skills. (https://www.apa.org/helpcenter/road-resilience.aspx).

Dealing with the fear of failure is not easy for most children, especially when they feel isolated from their peers due to bad grades, mobbing, exclusions or parental prohibitions. Negative thoughts such as "I can't do anything," "Nobody likes me/wants me" or "I am not allowed to do anything!" can be pictured by cartoons as faulty thinking. Alternative positive thoughts can be encouraged by examples, such as "What would a strong child or Batman do?" and "What am I still allowed to do?" Familiar problem-solving strategies as described in the ICPS program ("I Can Problem Solve," Shure, 2001) can be practiced in difficult situations.

Positive alternative thinking and associations of different solutions might even help in the case of major problems, such as *dealing with the loss* of an intact family, a beloved pet, friends or even the indispensable cell phone. It is self-understood that children will get support during difficult times.

LTG 5 Dealing with frustration and using coping strategies

STG 1 Dealing with the feelings of failure

- Dealing with the rejection of an application
- Dealing with lack of popularity
- Being the only one not allowed to join the field trip
- Being the only one not passing the bike exam

STG 2 Dealing with losses and thinking positively

- Divorce of parents
- Loss of a friend due to switching schools
- Loss of cell phone
- Loss of pet

Chart 6: LTG 5

NAME OF STUDENT: _____	CARTOON	ROLE-PLAYING	VIDEO-MODELING	DISCUSSION
DATE				
LTG 5 Dealing with frustration and using coping strategies				
STG 1 Dealing with the feelings of failure				
• Dealing with the rejection of an application				
• Dealing with lack of popularity				
• Being the only one not allowed to join the field trip				
• Being the only one not passing the bike exam				
STG 2 Dealing with losses and thinking positively				
• Divorce of parents				
• Loss of a friend due to switching schools				
• Loss of cell phone				
• Loss of pet				

LTG 5
Dealing with
frustration
and using
coping
strategies

5.1
Dealing with
feelings of
failure

Your application has been declined.
What do you think/say/do?

You are not very popular at school and notice your peers talking about you.
What do you think/say/do?

Your mom says that you are not allowed to join the field trip.
What do you think/say/do?

You are the only one who did not pass the bike exam.
What do you think/say/do?

LTG 5
Dealing with
frustration
and using
coping
strategies

5.2
Dealing with
losses and
thinking
positively

Your parents got divorced.
What do you think/say/do?

You switched schools and have lost your friends.
What do you think/say/do?

You lost your cell phone.
What do you think/say/do?

Your dog had to be put to sleep.
What do you think/say/do?

Hachiko was a dog who lived from 1923 until 1935 in a small town in Japan. He accompanied his owner daily to the train station and waited until he returned, even under harsh weather conditions. After the owner's death, Hachiko still waited expectantly at the train station for nine years. Hachiko's loyalty was honored by a statue and a movie in 2009 called *Hachiko*.

This example shows loyalty in animals which goes beyond the death of a loved one to whom they have been loyal. While loyalty contributes to stability and trust in a relationship, it seems to have gone out of fashion in recent years. Seventy years ago, war widows often spent the rest of their lives alone, not giving up hope in the return of their loved ones. Even unhappy marriages were often endured for a lifetime. Nowadays, short-term relationships, divorces or life-section partnerships have become more of a trend. Frequent moves, constant change of schools or jobs require flexibility in the long run. Still, even now, Hachiko's story obviously serves as an important reminder of loyalty and stability. More than seventy years after Hachiko's death, an annual ceremony takes place to honor him. The movie has been released in more than 50 countries.

Loyalty is a long-term commitment to a person, group, belief, nation or country. People can be loyal to their country of birth or their homeland. Loyalty is linked to the *integrity of a person*, which means being loyal to yourself. This entails the fidelity to oneself and continuous agreement of the personal value system with one's actions (Wikipedia).

A person is *trustworthy* if he is loyal, integrous, authentic, predictable and reliable over a long-term period. Many teenagers find it difficult *to be loyal* towards their parents or teachers. Instead, they try to get acceptance from peers by ridiculing the authority figures. Fictional stories about the parents' or teachers' embarrassing moments or strict parenting are considered "cool" among certain peer-groups. *(STG 1)*

Integrity is another component which belongs to a set of values from the Positive Behavior Support movements. Students can choose any of the character traits as the positive goal. During school hours, they can practice their selected goal. Being faithful to yourself entails not participating in dangerous or forbidden incitements and instead standing up for your opinion, even if this is not considered "cool." *(STG 2)*

Being honest even if you fear punishment or negative consequences is another important goal to build up trust. Here is a slogan which might help: "Everyone makes mistakes." It's not that bad as long as one admits them and tries to correct the mistakes or clarifies misunderstandings. Having a clear intention to learn from mistakes is also an important step *(STG 3)*.

In the following cartoons, we select possible goals to build up *trust and to develop integrity.*

LTG 6 Being loyal and trustworthy

STG 1 Being loyal

- Not making fun of your parents
- Respecting teachers
- Being loyal to lost loved ones
- Being loyal to your team

STG 2 Being real and self-confident

- Don't join in on instigating
- Don't join in when others are doing something dangerous
- Don't join in when others are doing something forbidden
- Expressing your own opinion and prevailing against the opinion of others

STG 3 Being honest even though you fear punishment or disadvantages

- Admitting that you damaged something
- Admitting that you stole something
- Admitting that you stole/borrowed money
- Admitting that you have made a mistake

Chart 7: LTG 6 Being loyal and trustworthy

NAME OF STUDENT: _____	CARTOON	ROLE-PLAYING	VIDEO-MODELING	DISCUSSION
DATE				
LTG 6 Being loyal and trustworthy				
STG 1 Being loyal				
• Not making fun of your parents				
• Respecting teachers				
• Apologize when making a mistake				
• Being loyal to your team				
STG 2 Being real and self-confident				
• Don't join in on instigating				
• Don't join in when others are doing something dangerous				
• Don't join in when others are doing something forbidden				
• Expressing your own opinion and prevailing against the opinion of others				

NAME OF STUDENT: _____	CARTOON	ROLE-PLAYING	VIDEO-MODELING	DISCUSSION
DATE				
STG 3 Being honest even though you fear punishment or disadvantages				
• Admitting when you damaged something				
• Admitting when you stole something				
• Admitting that you stole/borrowed money				
• Admitting that you have made a mistake				

LTG 6
Being loyal and trustworthy

6.1
Being loyal

Your mom accidently dropped ice cream on her shirt.
What do you think/say/do?

You have a new teacher.
What do you think/say/do?

LTG 6
Being
loyal and
trustworthy

6.1
Being loyal

Your parents want to go to the cemetery to bring flowers to your grandma.
What do you think/say/do?

Your team lost, and you are thinking about switching the teams.
What do you think/say/do?

LTG 6
Being
loyal and
trustworthy

6.2
Being real and
self-confident

Your friends want you to help spray-paint the wall before someone comes.
What do you think/say/do?

Your friends want you to cross a bridge that is not stable enough.
What do you think/say/do?

LTG 6
Being
loyal and
trustworthy

6.2
Being real and
self-confident

Your colleagues want you to take a hit with them.
What do you think/say/do?

You hear your classmates talking negatively about a movie.
What do you think/say/do?

LTG 6
Being
loyal and
trustworthy

6.3
Being honest
even though
you fear
punishment or
disadvantages

You spilled a glass of water onto the couch, and your mother asks who it was.
What do you think/say/do?

Your brother misses his cookies and asks you where they are.
What do you think/say/do?

LTG 6
Being
loyal and
trustworthy

6.3
Being honest
even though
you fear
punishment or
disadvantages

Your teacher asks the class who took the money out of the class cashbox.
What do you think/say/do?

Your teacher gave you your neighbor's exam back with a good grade.
What do you think/say/do?

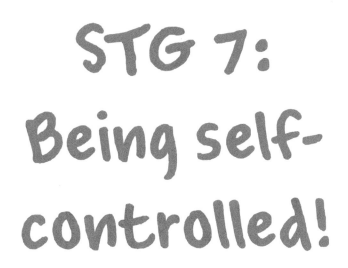

During the 60s, Walter Mitchel and Ebbe Ebenson (1970) from the Stanford University tested four to six year-old children. Children were given a marshmallow (or something similar) with the promise that they would receive a second one if they waited for the experiment to return. Out of a group of 600 children, one-third waited with significant efforts (smelling, licking, or touching the tempting sweet) up to fifteen minutes for the promised second marshmallow. The remaining two-thirds were impatient enough to eat the marshmallow immediately. The children who were able to wait for the second one showed positive social behavior and higher test results at the age of fifteen (Mitchel, 2015).

Even though follow-up results did not confirm the test's predictability of life success (Duncan, 2018), being able to delay satisfaction is an important component of self-control. According to long-term studies, self-discipline, conscientiousness and setting up long-term goals are important traits and behaviors for later mental health, wellbeing and satisfaction (Moffitt, T., Caspi, A., & Poulton, R., 2014). This chapter visualizes various traits of self-control.

Children should be instructed to practice *self-control*, which means observing and reflecting oneself and behaving accordingly. They should learn to follow personal long-term goals and related short-term goals. While it might be more fun to check out the latest news on Facebook than to finish homework, stable knowledge, better grades and improved job options are their long-term benefits.

"How do I act towards others?" The first step toward *evaluating yourself* is to *observe yourself*. "Is it possible that my actions, such as chewing on my nails or other idiosyncratic behaviors, annoy others?" *(STG 7.1)*

Another important social value is *being considerate*. "What do others expect of me?" "Which behavior might annoy or hurt someone?" Loud music might be relaxing to myself, but it might annoy others *(STG 7.1)*. Being considerate can even mean distorting the truth slightly to not disappoint someone (such as when you receive a gift you already have).

Individuals can manage *inappropriate behaviors* such as anger and temper outbursts through *self-control* methods. If students come home irritated because they received negative feedback or a bad grade, positive behavioral choices would include stress reduction and time management strategies *(STG 7.2)*. Instead of "freaking out," having a plan and managing tasks step by step are shown as a positive alternative *(STG 7.2)*.

From the large range of possible everyday situations, we have selected the following examples. As before, parents and teachers are invited to develop additional individual alternatives.

LTG 7 Being self-controlled

STG 1 Being aware of yourself and others

- Not annoying others with a monologue
- Not everyone thinks biting nails is cool
- Expressing stress at school (deliberate/intentionally)
- Being thoughtful

STG 2 Dealing with stress

- Using calming strategies while preparing for an exam
- Don't be angry when being bullied
- Dealing with weight

Chart 8: STG 7 Self control

NAME OF STUDENT:_____	CARTOON	ROLE-PLAYING	VIDEO-MODELING	DISCUSSION
DATE				
LTG 7 Being self-controlled				
STG 1 Being aware of yourself and others				
• Not annoying others with a monologue				
• Not everyone thinks biting nails is cool				
• Expressing stress at school (deliberate/ intentionally)				
• Being thoughtful				
STG 2 Dealing with stress				
• Using calming strategies while preparing for an exam				
• Don't be angry when being bullied				
• Dealing with weight				

LTG 7
Being self-controlled

7.1
Being aware of yourself and others

New cars fascinate you, but the others are not listening to you.
What do you think/say/do?

When you are nervous, you bite your nails.
What do you think/say/do?

LTG 7
Being self-controlled

7.1
Being aware
of yourself
and others

You come from school totally stressed out and throw your bag in the corner. Your mother asks you what is going on.
What do you think/say/do?

You walk through the park with your music and see an old man covering his ears.
What do you think/say/do?

LTG 7
Being self-controlled

7.2
Dealing with stress

You have an exam in two weeks and don't know where to start.
What do you think/say/do?

You see a negative comment on Facebook about you.
What do you think/say/do?

LTG 7
Being self-
controlled

7.2
Dealing
with stress

You love to eat sweets but barely fit into your favorite pants.
What do you think/say/do?

You have a concert tomorrow, but your friends want to go to the playground with you.
What do you think/say/do?

135

During recess, a group of teenagers sits together and listens to a monologue from their (autistic) peer. He describes in detail his fascination for black holes. Suddenly he stops and comments, "Oops, that was 'Me-talk' – I should have used 'You-talk' instead." He starts listening to the others and joins their less unusual topic.

Obviously, the practiced social and communicative program has helped the adolescent talk about the interests of others instead of mainly talking about his own interests. A requirement is to be self-observant and to consider the reactions of others, to one's behavior. In order to respond appropriately to others he must also take into account the facial expressions or postures of his interaction partners. The long-term goal is to be a competent communication partner with the above listed skills, such as considering the perspectives of others, walking in others' shoes and controlling oneself. We can assume that many friendships, marriages, or careers can be saved if targeted training in perspective-considering has been accomplished.

During the 80s, Carl Rogers developed "active listening," which is part of "Client-Centered Therapy" (Rogers, 1985). The main traits are being value-free and listening empathetically, which signals to the interaction partner complete acceptance of his personality, while holding back your own opinion.

Active listening is a common feature even outside of therapy sessions. The method is used in meditation, medicine, social work, law and other disciplines. Dispute Resolution programs at schools value active listening as a strategy for conflict solutions (https://www.bug-nrw.de/landesprogramm/).

Active listening is not always easy, so in the case of talking about a holiday, the listener often responds with talking about his own holiday experience instead of listening, commenting or asking about the other's experience. Children also should be sensitized to the emotions the interaction partner expresses. During emotional topics such as the good news of being accepted to a university or the concern about a grandma's health, active listening is especially a must *(STG 8.1)*.

The concept of "You- instead of Me-talk" will be better visualized through cartoons. The examples show that the others are uninterested in the self-compliments about soccer and the vast meanderings of family stories *(STG 8.2)*.

In general, it is easier for people to criticize others than to *give compliments*. Students or teachers are no exception. Teachers should have a praise-to-blame ratio of four praises to one critical comment. Students should also be reminded of appropriate praise (Myers, Simonsen & Sugai, 2011). Compliments can be made about external features, such as a new dress, the amazing music playlist or inner qualities, such as the helpfulness of others. Instead of envying the winner for his victory or your classmate for his better grades, examples are given of sincere compliments *(STG 8.3)*.

LTG 8 Being a good conversational partner

STG 1 Giving compliments

- About someone's clothes
- About someone's possession
- About someone's grade
- About someone's skills

STG 2 Apologizing and making up for mistakes

- Apologizing when hurting someone
- Apologizing when breaking something
- Apologizing when forgetting something
- Apologizing when being dishonest

STG 3 Clarifying misunderstandings

- Clarifying wrong information
- Clarifying misunderstandings
- Clarifying date for the next exam
- Clarifying a doctor's appointment

STG 4 "You-talk" instead of "Me-talk"

- Don't perseverate on your favorite subject
- Don't be a "show-off"
- Considering the interest of others
- Don't always insist on being right

STG 5 Showing interest towards others and paying attention

- Paying attention when success within the family is mentioned
- Paying attention when the loss of a family member is mentioned
- Paying attention when your friend is telling you about his vacation
- Paying attention to the joy of a friend

STG 6 Showing thankfulness

- For a dinner invitation
- For a trip
- For critical feedback
- For life advice

Chart 9: LTG 8 Being a good conversational partner

NAME OF STUDENT: _____	CARTOON	ROLE-PLAYING	VIDEO-MODELING	DISCUSSION
DATE				
LTG 8 Being a good conversational partner				
STG 1 Giving compliments				
• About someone's clothes				
• About someone's possession				
• About someone's grade				
• About someone's skills				
STG 2 Apologizing and making up for mistakes				
• Apologizing when hurting someone				
• Apologizing when breaking something				
• Apologizing when forgetting something				
• Apologizing when being dishonest				
STG 3 Clarifying misunderstandings				
• Clarifying wrong information				
• Clarifying misunderstandings				
• Clarifying date for the next exam				
• Clarifying a doctor's appointment				

NAME OF STUDENT: _____	CARTOON	ROLE-PLAYING	VIDEO-MODELING	DISCUSSION
DATE				
STG 4 "You-talk" instead of "Me-talk"				
• Don't perseverate on your favorite subject				
• Don't be a "show-off"				
• Considering the interest of others				
• Don't always insist on being right				
STG 5 Showing interest towards others and paying attention				
• Paying attention when success within the family is mentioned				
• Paying attention when the loss of a family member is mentioned				
• Paying attention when your friend is telling you about his vacation				
• Paying attention to the joy of a friend				
STG 6 Showing thankfulness				
• For a dinner invitation				
• For a trip				
• For critical feedback				
• For life advice				

LTG 8
Being a good
conversational
partner

8.1
Giving
compliments

Your friend is wearing a new dress.
What do you think/say/do?

Your friend shows you a new song on his iPod.
What do you think/say/do?

LTG 8
Being a good
conversational
partner

8.1
Giving
compliments

Your mother wants to see your exam.
What do you think/say/do?

Your classmate was the first to finish the race.
What do you think/say/do?

LTG 8
Being a good
conversational
partner

8.2
Apologizing
and making up
for mistakes

You accidently hit a little girl with your bike.
What do you think/say/do?

You are playing tag with your friend and bump into the vase.
What do you think/say/do?

COMICS for Social & Communicative Behavior

LTG 8
Being a good
conversational
partner

8.2
Apologizing
and making up
for mistakes

Your mother told you to go to the grocery store and get whipped
cream, but you forgot it.
What do you think/say/do?

Your mother found out that you did not go to orchestra practice.
What do you think/say/do?

149

LTG 8
Being a good
conversational
partner

8.3
Clarifying
misunder-
standings

You are 100% sure that Indian elephants have bigger ears, but your friend does not agree.
What do you think/say/do?

Your parents are talking about the Paris deal, but you don't know what that is.
What do you think/say/do?

LTG 8
Being a good
conversational
partner

8.3
Clarifying
misunder-
standings

Your teacher asks the class if they are prepared for the exam.
What do you think/say/do?

Your mother reminds you of your dentist appointment.
What do you think/say/do?

LTG 8
Being a good
conversational
partner

8.4
"You-talk"
instead of
"Me-talk"

You are fascinated by caves, but your friends are bored.
What do you think/say/do?

Your team and you won a game and you are proud of yourself.
What do you think/say/do?

LTG 8
Being a good
conversational
partner

8.4
"You-talk"
instead of
"Me-talk"

You start talking about your grandfather but nobody seems to listen.
What do you think/say/do?

You are certain that the closest planet to the sun is Venus.
What do you think/say/do?

LTG 8
Being a good
conversational
partner

8.5
Showing
interest
towards others
and paying
attention

Your sister is telling you about her confirmation for the university she wanted to attend.
What do you think/say/do?

Your friend is telling you that her grandmother is in the hospital.
What do you think/say/do?

LTG 8
Being a good
conversational
partner

8.5
Showing
interest
towards others
and paying
attention

Your best friend tells you about his ski trip.
What do you think/say/do?

Your friend tells you about her visit at the shelter.
What do you think/say/do?

LTG 8
Being a good
conversational
partner

8.6
Showing
thankfulness

Your parents invite you to dinner.
What do you think/say/do?

Your father wants to take you on a trip to the zoo.
What do you think/say/do?

LTG 8
Being a good
conversational
partner

8.6
Showing
thankfulness

A friend alerts you that your t-shirt is inside-out.
What do you think/say/do?

When you were younger, your grandmother told you something important which you remembered when you saw her again as a teenager.
What do you think/say/do?

Conclusion!

The cartoon book should be an inspiration to work on desirable social behaviors, virtues and values. The refreshing cartoons can serve as ice-breakers to discuss topics which may be considered too intrusive or "top-down sermons." Parents and teachers should not just focus on the cartoon examples, but also use these as an incentive for role-play or video modeling. A thorough discussion of the respective goals and related behaviors is considered of additional benefit.

The described long- and short-term goals are found in many social training programs, and even represent general expectations of college teachers and employers. A key work-life qualification is to behave politely or respectfully, to be reliable and responsible, and to have good time management and team skills. Adequate communication has a high priority, since constructive handling of criticism, clarification of misunderstandings, the ability to compromise and active listening are key qualities of good students and employees. These should be targeted during the school years.

Again, the following cartoon examples have been chosen from several possible training goals. These have emerged from the daily problems of teachers and parents of children in regular schools as well as professionals involved with children and teenagers with behavioral challenges. As mentioned before, the pictured examples should be used as starting points in the discussion about values. Schools should focus on proactive programs for values and regular targeted practice.

This book is not only useful for elementary schools, but also for a wide range of ages and abilities. For most of the goals, one would wish not only that students, parents and teachers focus on the above virtues and positive interactions, but also that public figures consider them a valuable guiding principle.

Literature!

Baker, J. E. (2004) Social skills training for children and adolescents with Asperger Syndrome and social-communicative problems, AAPC, Shawnee Mission, Kansas.

Bernard-Opitz, V. (2014) Visuelle Methoden in der Autismus-spezifischen Verhaltenstherapie (AVT): Das Cartoon und Skript-Curriculum zum Training von Sozialverhalten und Kommunikation, Kohlhammer-Verlag: Stuttgart.

Carr, E.G. et al (1999). Positive Behavior Support for People with Developmental Disabilities: A research synthesis, (Monographs American Association on Mental Retardation).

Cox, J. W. & Rich, S. (2018) Scarred by school shootings, Washington Post, https://www.washingtonpost.com/graphics/2018/local/us-school-shootings-history/?noredirect=on&utm_term=.c4f37612d731.

Dunlap, G., Sailor, W. Horner, R.H. & Sugai, G. (2009). Handbook of Positive Behavioral Support: Including people with difficult behavior in the community, Springer.

Giesecke, H. (2004). Was kann die Schule zur Werteerziehung beitragen? In: Gruehn, Sabine/Kluchert, Gerhard/Koinzer, Thomas (Hrsg.): Was Schule macht. Schule, Unterricht und Werteerziehung: theoretisch, historisch, empirisch. Weinheim/Basel 2004, 235-246.

Hackl, A. (2011). Konzepte schulischer Werteerziehung. In: Hackl, A. & Steenbuck, O. Werteerziehung in Schulen, Vortrag, ALP Dillingen. https://www.google.com/search?q=Werteerziehung+an+Schulen&ie=utf-8&oe=utf-8&client=firefox-b-1-ab.

Kern Koegel, L, Koegel, R. & L. Dunlap, G. (2001), *Positive Behavioral Support*. Brookes Publishing.

McGinnis, E. (2005) Skillstreaming in the elementary schools: Lesson plans and activities, Research Press. www.researchpress.com.

OCDE - Orange County Department of Education, Positive Behavior Intervention Support, http://www.ocde.us/PBIS/Pages/Articles-and-Research.aspx.

Shure, M.B. (2001). I Can Problem Solve: An Interpersonal Cognitive Problem Solving Program (ICPS), Research Press.

Simpson, R.G. & Allday, R.A. (2008). PIE-R2: The area of a circle and good behavior management. TEACHING Exceptional Children Plus, 4(4), 2-10.

Zuna, N. & McDougall, D. (2004). Break time: Using Positive Behavior Support to manage avoidance of academis tasks, Council for Exceptional Children, Teaching Exceptional Children, (37), 1, 18-24.

Carl R. Rogers: Die nicht-direktive Beratung. Counseling and Psychotherapy. Fischer, Frankfurt am Main 1985.

Myers, D. M. Simonson, B. & Sugai, G. (2011). Increasing teachers' use of praise with a response-to-intervention approach. Education and Treatment of Children, 34, 35-39.

Creator Bios

Vera Bernard-Opitz, Ph.D.

Vera Bernard-Opitz is an American BCBA-D and German psychotherapist and behavior therapist who has worked in Germany, Singapore and the U.S. She has assessed and treated more than 1,000 children with Autism Spectrum Disorders (ASD) in autism research centers, rehabilitation centers, special needs schools and homes.

She studied Psychology at the University of Göttingen, conducting her Ph.D research in Göttingen and the University of California Santa Barbara. For seven years, she headed the Psychological Services unit at a rehabilitation center near Heidelberg, where she set up behavioral programs for individuals with ASD. Her research on computer-assisted instruction was funded by the German Research Foundation (DFG).

For twelve years she was Associate Professor of Psychology at the National University of Singapore, mainly teaching Abnormal Psychology and Behavior Modification. During this period, she initiated the first autism program in Singapore (STEP), where she coordinated training and research activities at the Behavior Intervention Center of the university.

Here in Southern California, she has supervised home-programs for a private ABA-company. For the last eight years, she has been an international consultant, spearheading tele-health for individuals with behavior challenges and varying levels of capabilities.

She has written several books focusing on behavior intervention, curriculum development and social skills training. The fourth edition of her curriculum guide *Children and Adolescents with ASD* was recently published by Kohlhammer Publishing. Her cartoon-book *Teaching-Goals: Communication and Social Behavior* has just been published in German and is in manuscript in English by Future Horizons. She edited the Autism Concrete Series with eight published books from internationally recognized authors.

Vera Bernard-Opitz lives with her family most of the year in Irvine. She spends three to four months in her home in the nice city of Hildesheim, from where she gives practice workshops throughout Germany.

Specialties: Autism Specific Behavior Intervention (ABA, Precision Teaching, Visual Support, Cognitive Behavior Intervention), Autism Spectrum Disorders, ADHD, Self-Injurious Behavior, Curriculum-Development, Parent and Staff Training, Supervision, Tele-Consultation

http://www.verabernard.de/us_index.htm

email: verabernard@gmail.com

Andra Bernard

Andra is a bilingual graphic designer who grew up in Germany and Singapore. She has a background in speech pathology and has completed her training as a graphic designer. She creates cartoons and comics for social behavior and communication skills in her very distinctive style. She loves art and has illustrated specialist books for children in German, English and Spanish.

www.andrabernard.design

CPSIA information can be obtained
at www.ICGtesting.com
Printed in the USA
JSHW020923040421
13141JS00003B/5